Handy Washington Genealogy Handbook

Gary L. Morris

©2015 Gary L. Morris

ISBN-13: 978-1508404545

ISBN-10: 1508404542

Table of Contents

Notes

Genealogical Research in Washington

Even though Washington is one of the younger states in America, there is a wealth of genealogical records and resources available for tracing your family history there. Because of the abundance of information held at many different locations, tracking down the records for your ancestor can be an ominous task. Don't worry though, we know just where they are, and we'll show you which records you'll need, while helping you to understand:

1. What they are
2. Where to find them
3. How to use them

These records can be found both online and off, so we'll introduce you to online websites, indexes and databases, as well as brick-and-mortar repositories and other institutions that will help with your research in Washington. So that you will have a more comprehensive understanding of these records, we have provided a brief history of the "Evergreen State" to illustrate what type of records may have been generated during specific time periods. That information will assist you in pinpointing times and locations on which to focus the search for your Washington ancestors and their records.

A Brief History of Washington

The first people to inhabit Washington were Asians who crossed the Bering Strait approximately 9,000 years ago. They then entered North America by way of the Pacific Northwest. The earliest known evidence of them remains in Washington - a human skeleton and burned bison bones – which date from around 7000 BC.

Although there are undocumented accounts of explorers Sir Francis Drake and Juan de Fuca exploring the area in the late 16th century, the first Europeans on record to visit Washington were 18th century Spaniards, notably Juan Perez in 1774, who explored the coastline as far north as Alaska, and Bruno Heceta, whose men made the first landing in Washington at the mouth of the Hoh River. The excursion ended in tragedy however, as Indians captured their landing boat and killed the explorers.

While searching for a Northwest Passage, English captain James Cook arrived in the area in 1778. He was the first of many English traders and explorers attracted to the area due to its wealth of sea otters, whose fur was very valuable. George Vancouver, another Englishman, followed in 1792, mapping the area of Puget Sound and the Pacific Coast. The mouth of the Columbia River was discovered by American fur trader Robert Gray, and as the trade fur grew, many more traders moved into the area, most representing the Canadian North West Company and the British Hudson's Bay Company.

During this time American interest in the area was piqued, and President Thomas Jefferson commissioned an overland exploration expedition to investigate the area that France acquired in the Louisiana Purchase of 1803. The men who would lead the expedition, Meriwether Lewis and William Clark would become famous in their own right. After Lewis and Clark spotted the Pacific Ocean from the banks of the Columbia River in 1805, American and British traders began to follow their route into the area.

When Clark was asked in 1831 to return to the area from St. Louis to assist in instructing the Native Americans inn the area in the Christian religion, the churches responded accordingly, flooding the area with missionaries who would establish the first settlement at Waiilatpu in 1836.The Indians were not receptive to the proselytizing however, and hostilities to the missionaries grew, culminating in a massacre of 14 Americans in 1847.

An American provisional government embracing the entire Oregon country and extending as far as the region that is now British Columbia, Canada, had been established as early as 1843. After much diplomatic and military maneuvering, a US-Canada boundary along the 49th parallel was established in 1846. The area became Washington Territory in 1853. The first territorial governor, Isaac Stevens, who was also a US superintendent of Indian affairs, negotiated a series of treaties with the Northwest Indian tribes and established a system of reservations. The treaties only made the already tense situation with the Indians worse, leading to the Yakima War in 1855, a series of bloody uprisings by the Yakima, Cayuse, and Nisqualli, which were not suppressed until toward the end of the decade.

The discovery of gold in the Walla Walla area brought prosperity to the entire region, which was boosted by the completion of the Northern Pacific Railroad in 1883. The railroad encouraged immigration, and by 1890, Washington's population, only 23,955 in 1870, swelled to 357,232. Washington was an early champion of women's suffrage, yet after granting women the vote in 1883, the suffrage acts were declared unconstitutional in 1887.

Important Dates in Washington History

1775 - Bruno de Hezeta lands on the Washington coast and claims the area for Spain.

1805-1806 - Lewis and Clark enter Washington and stay at Fort Clatsop

1811 - Fort Astoria built at the mouth of the Columbia River as part of Pacific Fur Company

1825 - Hudson's Bay Company establishes forts Vancouver and Colvile

1831 - Department of Indian Affairs is set up in the Department of the Interior. New duties include dealing with Native American nations in the West.

1839 - Jesuit missions established in Washington and resent day Idaho.

1843 -The Great Migration -1,000 pioneers head out on the Oregon Trail

1848 - Oregon Territory created.

1851 - First settlers land on the site of Seattle.

1853 - Washington Territory created.

1855-58 - Yakima Indian War

1859 - Oregon joins the Union as a Free State.

1889 - Washington becomes the 42nd state.

1897-99 - Klondike Gold Rush; Seattle grows quickly as a jump-off point to gold fields

Famous Battles Fought in Washington

Washington's history has been a relatively peaceful one, except for the **Yakima War** during the 1850's.

Yakima War: http://www.legendsofamerica.com/wa-indianconflicts3.html

The battle accounts that exist can be very effective in uncovering the military records of your ancestor. They can tell you what regiments fought in which battles, and often include the names and ranks of many officers and enlisted men.

Common Washington Genealogical Issues and Resources to Overcome Them

Boundary Changes: Boundary changes are a common obstacle when researching Washington ancestors. You could be searching for an ancestor's record in one county when in fact it is stored in a different one due to historical county boundary changes.

The **Atlas of Historical County Boundaries** can help you to overcome that problem. It provides a chronological listing of every boundary change that has occurred in the history of Washington.

Atlas of Historical County Boundaries:
http://publications.newberry.org/ahcbp/documents/WA_Consolidate d_Chronology.htm#Consolidated_Chronology

Name Changes: Surname changes, variations, and misspellings can complicate genealogical research. It is important to check all spelling variations. Soundex, a program that indexes names by sound, is a useful first step, but you can't rely on it completely as some name variations result in different Soundex codes. The surnames could be different, but the first name may be different too. You can also find records filed under initials, middle names, and nicknames as well, so you will need to **get creative with surname variations** and spellings in order to cover all the possibilities. For help with surname variations read our instructional article on **How to Use Soundex**.

get creative with surname variations:
http://obituarieshelp.org/blog/?p=634

How to Use Soundex: http://obituarieshelp.org/blog/?p=505

Washington Genealogical Organizations and Archives

Genealogical resources include not only records, but the organizations that house them, or can direct you to them. These institutions include: *Archives, Libraries, Genealogical Societies, Family History Centers, Universities, Churches, and Museums.*

Following are links to their websites, their physical addresses, and a summary of the records you can find there.

Archives and Libraries

Washington State Archives – Vital records, City and County Directories, Court and Prison records, Gazetteers, Business directories, Military records, Historical maps and atlases, Historical newspapers, School census records, Territorial census records, Territorial Assessment Rolls

1129 Washington Street SE
Olympia, WA 98504

Mailing Address:

PO Box 40238
Olympia, Washington 98504-0238
E-mail:research@sos.wa.gov
Telephone:(360) 586-1492
Fax:(360) 664-8814

Washington State Archives:
http://www.sos.wa.gov/history/genealogy.aspx

Washington State Library - Biographies, Cemetery Transcriptions, Census Records, City & County Directories, City & County Histories, Gazetteers & Business Directories, Immigration Records, Land Records, Maps & Atlases, Military Records, Newspapers, Obituaries, Funeral Home Records

Point Plaza East
6880 Capitol Blvd. SE, Tumwater
Olympia WA 98504-2460
Tel: (360) 704-5200

Washington State Library:
http://www.sos.wa.gov/library/Genealogy.aspx

National Archives Pacific and Alaska Region (Seattle) - Federal population censuses for all States, 1790-1930 (including indexes for 1880, 1900, 1910, and 1920); military service records; pension and bounty land warrant applications; some passenger arrival and naturalization records; records relating to the Five Civilized Tribes.

6125 Sand Point Way, N.E.
Seattle, WA 98115-7999
Telephone: 206-336-5115
Fax: 206-336-5112

National Archives Pacific and Alaska Region:
http://www.archives.gov/seattle/public/

Suzzallo-Allen Library - Large collection of genealogical and historical resources

University of Washington
P.O. Box 352900
Seattle, WA 98195-2900
Telephone: 206-543-9158
Fax: 206-685-8049

Suzzallo-Allen Library :
http://www.lib.washington.edu/types/collections

Genealogical and Historical Societies

Genealogical and historical societies have access to extensive catalogues of genealogical data. They are also able to offer expert guidance for genealogical researchers. Many members are professional genealogists who are most willing to share their expertise in finding ancestors.

Washington State Genealogical Society – Cemetery records, Pioneers list and many more genealogical resources for searching Washington ancestors

1901 S. 12th Avenue,
Union Gap, WA 98903-1256

Washington State Genealogical Society: http://www.wasgs.org/

Washington State Historical Society – Large genealogical library specializing in Women's history

1911 Pacific Avenue
Tacoma, WA 98402
Toll-free 1-888-BE THERE (1-888-238-4373)

Washington State Historical Society:
http://www.washingtonhistory.org/

Seattle Genealogical Society – Variety of resources including Irish and German interest groups, rare books, pioneer family records, periodicals, Seattle City directories, Washington State Death Index 1907-1989, Surname index

6200 Sand Point Way NE. Seattle

Mailing Address:
P.O Box 15329
Seattle, WA 98115-0329

Seattle Genealogical Society:
http://www.seattlegenealogicalsociety.org/

Additional Washington Genealogy Resources

Washington Mailing Lists

Mailing lists are internet based facilities that use email to distribute a single message to all who subscribe to it. When information on a particular surname, new records, or any other important genealogy information related to the mailing list topic becomes available, the subscribers are alerted to it. Joining a mailing list is an excellent way to stay up to date on Washington genealogy research topics. Rootsweb have an extensive listing of **Washington Mailing Lists** on a variety of topics.

Washington Mailing Lists:
http://lists.rootsweb.ancestry.com/index/usa/WA/misc.html

Washington Message Boards

A message board is another internet based facility where people can post questions about a specific genealogy topic and have it answered by other genealogists. If you have questions about a surname, record type, or research topic, you can post your question and other researchers and genealogists will help you with the answer. Be sure to check back regularly, as the answers are not emailed to you. The Washington message boards at **Rootsweb** are completely free to use.

Rootsweb:
http://boards.rootsweb.com/localities.northam.usa.states/mb.ashx

Washington Newspapers and Periodicals

Many genealogy periodicals and historical newspapers contain reprinted copies of family genealogies, transcripts of family Bible records, information about local records and archives, census indexes, church records, queries, land records, obituaries, court records, cemetery records, and wills. The following sites have historical Washington newspapers and periodicals that you can search online or on-site.

Washington State Library - Washington State newspapers dating from 1853 – present

Point Plaza East
6880 Capitol Blvd. SE, Tumwater
Olympia WA 98504-2460
Tel: (360) 704-5200

Washington State Library:
http://www.sos.wa.gov/library/Genealogy.aspx

Seattle Genealogical Society – Periodicals from all of the United States, Canada, the United Kingdom, Scandinavia, and other international regions.

6200 Sand Point Way NE. Seattle

Mailing Address:
P.O Box 15329
Seattle, WA 98115-0329

Seattle Genealogical Society:
http://www.seattlegenealogicalsociety.org/

GenealogyBank.com – free searchable database of Washington newspaper archives, 1890-1984

GenealogyBank.com:
http://www.genealogybank.com/gbnk/newspapers/explore/USA/Washington/

The Online Books Page – links to historical Washington books and periodicals available for viewing online

The Online Books Page link to:
http://onlinebooks.library.upenn.edu/

Library of Congress Digital Newspaper Directory – free searchable database of historical U.S. newspapers dating from 1690-present

Library of Congress Digital Newspaper Directory:
http://chroniclingamerica.loc.gov/search/titles/

NewspaperArchive.com – largest online database of historical newspapers in the world.

NewspaperArchive.com: http://newspaperarchive.com/

Historical Wahington Maps and Gazetteers

Maps are an integral part of genealogical research. They help us to
locate landmarks, towns, cities, parishes, states, provinces,
waterways and roads and streets. They also help us to determine
when and where boundary changes might have taken place, and give
us a visualization of the area we're researching in.

For locating place names, a gazetteer is the best possible resource for
any genealogist. Gazetteers are also sometimes called "place name
dictionaries", and can help you to locate the area in which you need
to conduct research. Below are links to the maps and gazetteers for
research in Washington.

Peabody GNIS Service – Washington:
http://peabody.research.yale.edu/cgi-
bin/Query.GNIS?ST=Washington&SU=1

Color Landform Atlas – Washington:
http://fermi.jhuapl.edu/states/wa_0.html

1985 U.S. Atlas: http://www.livgenmi.com/1895/WA/

Washington Hometown Locator:
http://washington.hometownlocator.com/

Washington State Library – Variety of gazetteers including:
Pacific Coast Business (1867), Disturnell's Business Directory and
Gazetteer of the West Coast of North America (1882), McKenney's
Pacific Coast Directory (1883-4, 1886-7), and Oregon, Washington
and Idaho Gazetteer and Business Directory (1886-7, 1892).

Point Plaza East
6880 Capitol Blvd. SE, Tumwater
Olympia WA 98504-2460
Tel: (360) 704-5200

Washington State Library:
http://www.sos.wa.gov/library/Genealogy.aspx

Washington City Directories

City directories are similar to telephone directories in that they list the residents of a particular area. The difference though is what is important to genealogists, and that is they pre-date telephone directories. You can find an ancestor's information such as their street address, place of employment, occupation, or the name of their spouse. A one-stop-shop for finding city directories in Washington is the **Washington Online Historical Directories** which contains a listing of every available online historical directory related to Washington. Another useful site is **US City Directories** which identifies printed, microfilmed, and online Washington directories and their repositories.

Washington Online Historical Directories: https://sites.google.com/site/onlinedirectorysite/Home/usa/wa

US City Directories: http://www.uscitydirectories.com/sd.htm

Washington State Archives – Extensive collection of City Directories for 35 Washington Counties and 300 cities dating from 1890 to present

1129 Washington Street SE
Olympia, WA 98504

Mailing Address:

PO Box 40238
Olympia, Washington 98504-0238
E-mail:research@sos.wa.gov
Telephone:(360) 586-1492
Fax:(360) 664-8814

Washington State Archives:
http://www.sos.wa.gov/history/genealogy.aspx

Washington Genealogical Records

Birth, Death, Marriage and Divorce Records – Also known as vital records, birth, death, and marriage certificates are the most basic, yet most important records attached to your ancestor. The reason for their importance is that they not only place your ancestor in a specific place at a definite time, but potentially connect the individual to other relatives. Below is a list of repositories and websites where you can find Washington vital records.

Washington State Department of Health - Birth and Death certificates from 1907-present, Marriage and Divorce certificated from 1968 - present

Center for Health Statistics
Town Center 1
101 Israel Road SE
Tumwater, WA 98501

Washington State Department of Health:
http://www.doh.wa.gov/LicensesPermitsandCertificates/BirthDeath MarriageandDivorce/AboutCertificates.asp

Washington State Archives – Birth and Death Registers, 1891-1907, Birth Records Index, 1907-1929, Death Records Index, 1907-2004, Divorce Records Index , 1968-2004, Marriage and Divorce Records, pre-1968, Marriage Records Index , 1968-2004

1129 Washington Street SE
Olympia, WA 98504

Mailing Address:
PO Box 40238
Olympia, Washington 98504-0238
E-mail:research@sos.wa.gov
Telephone:(360) 586-1492
Fax:(360) 664-8814

Washington State Archives:
http://www.sos.wa.gov/history/genealogy.aspx

Family Search has the following indexes that can be searched online for free:

Washington, County Deaths, 1891-1907:
https://familysearch.org/search/collection/1389738

Washington, County Divorce Records, 1852-1950:
https://familysearch.org/search/collection/1930340

Washington, County Marriages, 1855-2008:
https://familysearch.org/search/collection/1534448

Washington, County Records, 1856-2009:
https://familysearch.org/search/collection/1910364

Washington, Death Certificates, 1907-1960:
https://familysearch.org/search/collection/1454923

Washington, King County Delayed Births, 1941-1942:
https://familysearch.org/search/collection/1463676

Washington, Pierce County Marriage Returns, 1891-1950:
https://familysearch.org/search/collection/1924073

Census Records

Census records are among the most important genealogical documents for placing your ancestor in a particular place at a specific time. Like BDM records, they can also lead you to other ancestors, particularly those who were living under the authority of the head of household.

Washington State Archives – Territorial census records 1857 – 1892, Territorial Assessment Rolls, 1857, 1860, 1874, and 1875, School census records

1129 Washington Street SE
Olympia, WA 98504

Mailing Address:

PO Box 40238
Olympia, Washington 98504-0238
E-mail:research@sos.wa.gov
Telephone:(360) 586-1492
Fax:(360) 664-8814

Washington State Archives:
http://www.sos.wa.gov/history/genealogy.aspx

Washington State Library - Washington Territorial Census Rolls, 1859-1892, Federal Census 1850 – 1880 and 1900 - 1930.

Point Plaza East
6880 Capitol Blvd. SE, Tumwater
Olympia WA 98504-2460
Tel: (360) 704-5200

Washington State Library:
http://www.sos.wa.gov/library/Genealogy.aspx

National Archives Pacific and Alaska Region (Seattle) - Federal population censuses for all States, 1790-1930 (including indexes for 1880, 1900, 1910, and 1920)

6125 Sand Point Way, N.E.
Seattle, WA 98115-7999
Telephone: 206-336-5115
Fax: 206-336-5112

National Archives Pacific and Alaska Region:
http://www.archives.gov/seattle/public/

The **Free Census Project** has transcribed many Washington indexes and new material is added daily

Free Census Projec: http://usgwcensus.org/cenfiles/wa.htm

Access Genealogy – Washington county census records dating from 1849

Access Genealogy:
http://www.accessgenealogy.com/census/washington-census-records.htm

African American Census Schedules Online – slave schedules, mortality schedules, slave-owners census

African American Census Schedules Online:
http://www.afrigeneas.com/aacensus/ga/

Native Americans in Census Records (US National Archives):
http://www.archives.gov/research/census/native-americans/

<u>Washington Church Records</u>

Church and synagogue records are a valuable resource, especially for baptisms, marriages, and burials that took place before 1900. You will need to at least have an idea of your ancestor's religious denomination, and in most cases you will have to visit a brick and mortar establishment to view them.

Most church records are kept by the individual church, although in some denominations, records are placed in a regional archive or maintained at the diocesan level. Local Historical Societies are sometimes the repository for the state's older church records. Below are links archives that maintain church records, as well as a few databases that can be viewed online.

The **Family History Library** contains many church records from a variety of denominations on microfilm.

Family History Library:
http://familysearch.org/learn/wiki/en/Family_History_Library

Central Repositories for Denominational Records

<u>Church of Jesus Christ of Latter-day Saints (Mormons)</u>

Early Mormon Church records for Washington can be found on film located at the LDS Family History Library in Salt Lake City and can be searched via the **Family History Library Catalog**

Family History Library Catalog:
https://familysearch.org/eng/Library/FHLC/frameset_fhlc.asp

The **Church History Library** has an even broader collection of historical church records than the Family History Library.
Church History Library
15 East North Temple
Salt Lake City, Utah 84150-1600
Phone: (801) 240-2272
Church History Library:
https://history.lds.org/?lang=eng#FlashPluginDetected

Central Repositories for Denominational Records

Baptist

American Baptist - Samuel Colgate Historical Library
1106 South Goodman Street
Rochester, NY 14620-2532
Phone: (716) 473-1740
Fax: (716) 473-1740

American Baptist - Samuel Colgate Historical Library:
http://abhsarchives.org/

Congregational

Congregational Library
14 Beacon Street
Boston, MA 02108
Phone: (617) 523-0470
Fax: (617) 523-0470

Congregational Library: http://www.14beacon.org/

Presbyterian

Presbyterian Historical Society
425 Lombard Street
Philadelphia, PA 19147
Telephone: 1-215-627-1852
Fax: 1-215-627-0509

Presbyterian Historical Society: http://www.history.pcusa.org/

Roman Catholic

Archdiocese of Seattle
Chancery Office
910 Marion Street
Seattle, WA 98104
Phone: (206) 382-4560
Fax: (206) 382-4840

Archdiocese of Seattle:
http://www.seattlearchdiocese.org/Archives/default.aspx

Diocese of Spokane
P.O. Box 1453
1023 W. Riverside Ave.
Spokane, WA 99210-1453
Phone: (509) 358-7300

Diocese of Spokane: http://www.dioceseofspokane.org/

Diocese of Yakima
5301-A Tieton Drive
Yakima, WA 98908-3493
Phone: (509) 965-7117

Diocese of Yakima: http://yakimadiocese.org/offices/chancery

Washington Military Records

More than 40 million Americans have participated in some kind of war service since America was colonized. The chance of finding your ancestor amongst those records is exceptionally high. Military records can even reveal individuals who never actually served, such as those who registered for the two World Wars but were never called to duty. Below are a number of links to websites and archives that contain Washington military records.

Washington State Archives – Serviceman cards, bonus applications, or rosters from the Indian War, Civil War, World War I, World War II, Korean War, and Vietnam War, Admissions files for the Orting Soldiers' Home, 1891-1987, and Retsil Veterans' Home, 1910-1992

1129 Washington Street SE
Olympia, WA 98504

Mailing Address:
PO Box 40238
Olympia, Washington 98504-0238
E-mail:research@sos.wa.gov
Telephone:(360) 586-1492
Fax:(360) 664-8814

Washington State Archives:
http://www.sos.wa.gov/history/genealogy.aspx

National Archives Pacific and Alaska Region (Seattle) - Military service records; pension and bounty land warrant applications

6125 Sand Point Way, N.E.
Seattle, WA 98115-7999
Telephone: 206-336-5115
Fax: 206-336-5112

National Archives Pacific and Alaska Region:
http://www.archives.gov/seattle/public/

National Archives and Records Administration - World War I
Draft Registration Cards
Microfilm Roll List

8601 Adelphi Road
College Park, MD 20740-6001
Toll free: 1-866-272-6272

National Archives and Records Administration:
http://www.archives.gov/research/military/

**US Department of Veterans Affairs Nationwide Gravesite
Locator** – includes information on veterans and their family
members buried in veterans and military cemeteries having a
government grave marker.

**US Department of Veterans Affairs Nationwide Gravesite
Locator**: http://gravelocator.cem.va.gov/

You may also find your ancestor's military records in the following
databases:

United States General Index to Pension Files, 1861-1934:
https://familysearch.org/search/collection/1919699

United States Index to Service Records, War with Spain, 1898:
https://familysearch.org/search/collection/1919583

United States Index to Indian Wars Pension Files, 1892-1926 –
military pension records of soldiers who fought in the Indian Wars
between 1817 and 1898

United States Index to Indian Wars Pension Files, 1892-1926:
https://familysearch.org/search/collection/1979427

United States Registers of Enlistments in the U.S. Army, 1798-1914 - index of men who enlisted in the United States Army, 1798-1914.

United States Registers of Enlistments in the U.S. Army, 1798-1914: https://familysearch.org/search/collection/1880762

United States Mexican War Pension Index, 1887-1926 - index to Mexican War pension files for service between 1846 and 1848

United States Mexican War Pension Index, 1887-1926: https://familysearch.org/search/collection/1979390

Civil War Soldiers Service Records - Service records for both Union and Confederate soldiers indexed by soldier's name, rank, and unit.

Civil War Soldier Service Records: http://go.fold3.com/civilwar_records/

Washington Cemetery Records

As convenient as it is to search cemetery records online, keep in mind that there are a few disadvantages over visiting a cemetery in person. They are:

- Tombstone information is not always accurately transcribed
- The arrangement of the graves in a cemetery can be crucial as family members are often buried next to each other or in the same grave. This arrangement is not always preserved in the alphabetical indexes that are found online.

With that information in mind, the following websites have databases that can be searched online for Washington Cemetery records.

Washington Tombstone Transcription Project - death and burial records

Washington Tombstone Transcription Project:
http://www.usgwtombstones.org/washington/

Washington State Library - Collection of cemetery transcriptions published by local genealogical and historical societies in Washington State

Point Plaza East
6880 Capitol Blvd. SE, Tumwater
Olympia WA 98504-2460
Tel: (360) 704-5200

Washington State Library:
http://www.sos.wa.gov/library/Genealogy.aspx

Washington State Genealogical Society – Variety of cemetery records covering the entire state of Washington

1901 S. 12th Avenue,
Union Gap, WA 98903-1256

Washington State Genealogical Society:
http://www.wasgs.org/cemeteryRecords.php

African American Cemeteries Online – African American, slave, and Native American cemetery records

African American Cemeteries Online:
http://africanamericancemeteries.com/

Access Genealogy – database of Washington cemetery record transcriptions

Access Genealogy:
http://www.accessgenealogy.com/cemetery/washington-cemetery-records.htm

Find a Grave – over 100 million grave records can be searched on this site. Search can be conducted by name, location, or cemetery name.

Find a Grave: http://www.findagrave.com/

Interment.net - A free online database containing approximately 4 million cemetery records from around the world.

Interment.net: http://www.interment.net/

Billion Graves – as the name implies, you can search a billion records including headstone photos, transcriptions, cemetery records, and grave locations.

Billion Graves:
http://billiongraves.com/pages/search/index.php#cemetery

<u>Washington Obituaries</u>

Obituaries can reveal a wealth about our ancestor and other relatives. You can search our **Washington Obituaries Listings** from hundreds of Washington newspapers online for free.

Washington Obituaries Listings:
http://obituarieshelp.org/washington_newspaper_obituaries.html

Washington Wills and Probate Records

The documents found in a probate packet may include a complete inventory of a person's estate, newspaper entries, witness testimony, a copy of a will, list of debtors and creditors, names of executors or trustees, names of heirs. They can not only tell you about the ancestor you're currently researching, but lead to other ancestors.

Washington State Archives – Territorial District Court probate case abstracts

1129 Washington Street SE
Olympia, WA 98504

Mailing Address:

PO Box 40238
Olympia, Washington 98504-0238
E-mail:research@sos.wa.gov
Telephone:(360) 586-1492
Fax:(360) 664-8814

Washington State Archives:
http://www.sos.wa.gov/history/genealogy.aspx

Family Search has the following indexes that can be searched online for free:

Washington, County Probate Case Files, 1832-1950:
https://familysearch.org/search/collection/1454946

Washington, County Probate Records, 1853-1929:
https://familysearch.org/search/collection/1979435

Washington, King County Probate Records, 1854-1927:
https://familysearch.org/search/collection/1878788

Washington Immigration and Naturalization Records

The naturalization process generated many types of records, including petitions, declarations of intention, and oaths of allegiance. These records can provide family historians with information such as a person's birth date and place of birth, immigration year, marital status, spouse information, occupation, witnesses' names and addresses, and more.

If your ancestor lived in or near a large city, or near a city where U.S. courts convened, you may find naturalization records in the **U.S. District Court** before 1906.

U.S. District Court:
http://www.uscourts.gov/FederalCourts/UnderstandingtheFederalCourts/DistrictCourts.aspx

For the rural areas of Washington, naturalization records may be found with the **County Courts** in each county. Often the records were mixed in with other court proceedings making them difficult to locate. A few counties kept separate records for naturalization. After 1906, all naturalizations were handled in Federal District Courts.

County Courts:
http://www.50states.com/washington/state_courts.htm

Washington State Archives – Declarations of Intent, Naturalization Certificates, Certificate Receipts, Naturalization Records, Petitions for Naturalizations dating from mid-19th century

PO Box 40238
Olympia, Washington 98504-0238
E-mail:research@sos.wa.gov
Telephone:(360) 586-1492
Fax:(360) 664-8814

Washington State Archives:
http://www.sos.wa.gov/history/genealogy.aspx

National Archives Pacific and Alaska Region (Seattle) - Some passenger arrival and naturalization records

6125 Sand Point Way, N.E.
Seattle, WA 98115-7999
Telephone: 206-336-5115
Fax: 206-336-5112

National Archives Pacific and Alaska Region:
http://www.archives.gov/seattle/public/

US National Archives – Immigration records, Naturalization records, Ship's Passenger lists

The National Archives and Records Administration
8601 Adelphi Road
College Park, MD 20740-6001
Tel: 1-866-272-6272; 1-86-NARA-NARAS

US National Archives: http://www.archives.gov/research/guide-fed-records/groups/085.html

Family Search has the following indexes which can be searched online for free:

Washington, County Naturalization Records, 1850-1982:
https://familysearch.org/search/collection/1932554

Washington, Seattle, Passenger Lists, 1890-1957:
https://familysearch.org/search/collection/1916081

Washington Native American Records

Leota Junior High Library – Washington State Indigenous Peoples Collection – includes; American Indians of the Pacific Northwest Collection, Bureau of Indian Affairs records, Washington State Governor's Office of Indian Affairs, Tribal histories, Nations, Confederations, and Reservations records, and much more

19301 168th Avenue NE
Woodinville, WA 98072
Tel: 425-408-6500

Leota Junior High Library:
http://webold.nsd.org//education/components/scrapbook/default.php?sectiondetailid=69663

Washington State Digital Archives – Indian Census records:
http://www.digitalarchives.wa.gov/Collections#RSID:37

National Archives Pacific and Alaska Region (Seattle) - Records relating to the Five Civilized Tribes

6125 Sand Point Way, N.E.
Seattle, WA 98115-7999
Telephone: 206-336-5115
Fax: 206-336-5112

National Archives Pacific and Alaska Region :
http://www.archives.gov/seattle/public/

National Archives and Records Administration - Dawes Commission Final Cards of the Five Civilized Tribes

8601 Adelphi Road
College Park, MD 20740-6001
Toll free: 1-866-272-6272

National Archives and Records Administration:
http://www.archives.gov/research/military/

Access Genealogy – Washington Native American census records, tribal histories, and much more

Access Genealogy:
http://www.accessgenealogy.com/native/washington-indian-tribes.htm

U.S. National Archives - information on American Indians who maintained their ties to Federally-recognized Tribes (1830-1970).

U.S. National Archives : http://www.archives.gov/research/native-americans/

Records of the Bureau of Indian Affairs (BIA):
http://www.archives.gov/research/guide-fed-records/groups/075.html

American Indians Records Repository - records dating from the 1700s including trust, education and other historic Indian Affairs records

American Indian Records Repository
Meritex Enterprises
17501 West 98th Street
Lenexa, KS 66219
Phone: 913-888-0601

American Indians Records Repository:
http://www.doi.gov/ost/records_mgmt/american-indian-records-repository.cfm

Missing Matriarchs – Resources for Researching Female Washington Ancestors

Looking for female ancestors requires an adjustment of how we view traditional records sources. A woman's identity was often under that of her husband, and often individual records for them can be difficult to locate. The following resources are effective in locating female ancestors in Washington where traditional records may not reveal them.

Bibliographies

- *Woman's Place: A Guide to Seattle and King County History,* Mildred T. Andrews (Gemil Press, 1994)
- *Northwest Women: An Annotated Bibliography of Sources on the History of Oregon and Washington Women, 1787-1970,* Karen J. Blair (Washington State University Press, 1997)
- *On Sidesaddles to Heaven: The Women on the Rocky Mountain Mission,* Laurie M. Carlson (Caxton Printers, 1998)
- *Seattle's Black Victorians, 1852-1901,* Esther Hale Mumford (Anase Press, 1980)
- *Women and Their Quilts: A Washington State Centennial Tribute,* Nancyann J. Twelker (That Patchwork Place, 1988)

Selected Resources for Washington Women's History

Women's History Consortium
1911 Pacific Avenue
Tacoma, WA 98402
Toll-free 1-888-BE THERE (1-888-238-4373)

Coalition for Women's History
Washington State University
History department
Pullman, WA 99164

Washington State Library
Washington Northeast Collection
PO Box 42460
Olympia, WA 99164-7204

Notes

Notes

www.ingramcontent.com/pod-product-compliance
Lightning Source LLC
Chambersburg PA
CBHW070512290526
45790CB00003B/1206